Wild Tales

Instructor's Handbook

SpellingYouSee.

Building Confidence

888-854-6284
spellingyousee.com
sales@demmelearning.com

Wild Tales Instructor's Handbook

©2020 Spelling You See

©2013 Karen J. Holinga, PhD

Published and distributed by Demme Learning

spellingyousee.com

1-888-854-6284 or +1 717-283-1448 | demmelearning.com

Lancaster, Pennsylvania USA

ISBN 978-1-60826-606-7

Revision Code 0322-B

Printed in the United States of America by Innovative Technologies in Print.

For information regarding CPSIA on this printed material call: 1-888-854-6284
and provide reference #0322-030922

1   14   1014

Table of Contents

Individual Lesson Instruction

Online Resources

Visit spellingyousee.com for videos and downloads to support your Wild Tales lessons.

About Spelling You See

The Spelling You See approach allows students to develop spelling skills at their own pace. The instructor directs, supports, and encourages students throughout the program. There are no weekly spelling lists or spelling tests and minimal instructor preparation. Instead, brief daily activities help students integrate writing, reading, spelling, speaking, and listening. As a result, students develop a long-term visual memory for everyday words.

Philosophy

All learners move through five developmental stages as they learn to spell. The core activities in Spelling You See allow students to progress sequentially through these stages. These five core activities are reading, listening, chunking, copywork, and dictation. Students complete these activities using the provided passages. This allows students to learn the spelling of words in a meaningful context.

If your student is new to Spelling You See, take a little more time with the first few lessons. Reading through this Handbook is essential to understanding the program and will contribute to achieving the most success. Be sure to watch the online videos to learn how to complete the core activities most effectively.

Visit **spellingyousee.com** for more information about the research behind the Spelling You See philosophy and approach and the developmental stages of spelling .

About *Wild Tales*

This level focuses on the skill development stage of spelling. This stage is one of the longest and most critical stages of developing spelling confidence. It can take up to four years or more to move through this stage.

Wild Tales contains thirty-six lessons divided between two student workbooks. Each lesson features a nonfiction passage about a different animal. These passages help students build their vocabulary and learn how to spell words in an interesting context.

Each lesson is divided into five parts, A through E. In the Student Workbook, a day's work consists of completing one of these parts. Each day, the instructor guides the student through the indicated activities. These activities are explained in depth throughout this handbook. Videos are also available on the website that demonstrate each activity.

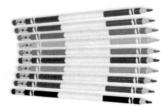

Wild Tales Instructor's Handbook

This Handbook should be the instructor's first stop each day, with tips about daily activities, lesson-by-lesson instructions, FAQs, and solutions.

Wild Tales Student Workbook, Parts 1 and 2

The Workbooks include thirty-six weekly lessons broken into five parts each, A–E. Each two- or four-page spread includes a checklist of that day's three activities.

Colored Pencils, Highlighters, or Crayons

Erasable colored pencils, included in the Universal Set or Student Pack, provide vivid color chunks that create a visual link with correct spelling. We recommend erasable pencils because they allow students to correct their work. However, highlighters or crayons can also be used. You will need yellow, purple, blue, pink or red, green, and orange.

The Wild Tales Universal Set includes all of the above items, plus:

Digital Tools (online)

The purchase of an Instructor's Handbook gives you access to online videos demonstrating daily activities, a symbol-coded answer key for those with color vision deficiency, and other useful downloads.

Add a pencil with an eraser and you're ready to go. Spelling You See is different, but it's not difficult. If you follow the program as detailed in this Handbook, your student will soon be on their way to becoming a more competent, confident speller.

For younger students, we also recommend:

Guide to Handwriting (optional add-on)

While this program is not a handwriting program, some young students may not be completely comfortable with writing. This laminated guide provides traceable letters for easy practice.

Lesson Structure

Each weekly lesson follows the same combination of activities, with a new passage and letter patterns. Instruction for each lesson begins with a chart like the one below. From this, you can quickly see which activities are to be completed and which letter patterns are the focus. You and your student will quickly fall into the rhythm of the lessons.

	Worksheet A	Worksheet B	Worksheet C	Worksheet D	Worksheet E
📖 Shared Reading	✓	✓	✓	✓	✓
💬 Chunking					
✏️ Copywork	⏱ 10 min	⏱ 10 min	⏱ 10 min		
✨ No Rule Day				✓	
🔊 Dictation					⏱ 10 min

Following the chart, you'll find details and things to watch for in that week's lesson. An activity may not have any notes if there is nothing unusual to do or watch for that week.

📖 Every Worksheet: Shared Reading, Chunking

Read the passage on the left-hand page together, following these directions carefully. First you will read the passage aloud (regardless of your student's reading ability). Then your student reads it aloud to you as you both follow along.

Your student will then "chunk" the passage, which means marking the letter patterns indicated in the instructions for that day. Most letter patterns have reference boxes on the Student Workbook pages that show the chunks to be marked and the color to be used, so there's no need to memorize the chunks.

✏️ Worksheet A–C: Copywork

Lesson-specific instruction and tips are included in this Handbook for each lesson. These instructions include suggestions about how to handle potentially confusing words or situations.

✨ Worksheet D: No Rule Day

Time to have fun and create! There are suggestions for No Rule Day activities on page 9 to get you started.

🔊 Worksheet E: Dictation

Set the timer, then dictate the passage as your student writes. Do this for just ten minutes–no more! After ten minutes, stop and count the number of words written. Even words the student needed help with should be counted as correct.

Details on the activities and how they should be completed begin on the next page.

Spelling You See is not difficult, but it is different. How does copywork help with spelling? What about reading aloud? The five core activities that make up the program may not all seem to directly relate to spelling. However, the skills used in these activities are the same as those needed for success in other language-related subjects, and they work best when they are strengthened together. There is no quick way through the skill development stage. The research supporting Spelling You See shows that it may take more than four years to develop visual memory and spelling confidence. Students will make small gains that add up to success, but it will almost certainly not happen overnight. Here is more information about each of the activities plus tips on how to set your student up for the most success possible. The lesson-by-lesson instructions beginning on page 12 include details unique to each lesson.

Shared Reading

At this level, some students are reading well and some are still developing their reading skills. While your student may be getting comfortable with reading, they may not be an expert yet. This is to be expected and is okay!

- Each day's activities in *Wild Tales* begin with reading the passage out loud to your student, regardless of their reading ability. They will then read it aloud to you while you provide as much help as necessary. Even if your student is a confident reader, do not skip this step. It is important for them to hear and read the passage exactly as it is written. Hearing them read it back to you is the best way to ensure that this happens.

- By listening to you read the passage before reading it out loud themselves, students are exposed to the correct pronunciation of new and irregularly-spelled words. Listening to the passage helps to emphasize beginning sounds and letters.

- The short, informational passages in *Wild Tales* include carefully researched, interesting facts about the selected animal of the week. The content introduces non-phonetic and high frequency words in an interesting context.

- The passages are intentionally written to be below the student's reading level so they can focus on the activities and not struggle with the reading.

Rule Breakers:

Discuss the non-phonetic word parts—the rule breakers—as you go. Show students how tricky the *gh* chunk is. This consonant chunk appears in words like *light*, *enough*, and *ghost*. *Ugh*! The *ai* chunk appears in *rain*, *again*, *said*, and *captain*. The word *house* has a silent *e* at the end, just to make it "look right." This is why "sounding out" a word is often not helpful and why Spelling You See does not teach spelling "rules" at the skill development stage. English spelling rules are inconsistent. Acknowledging this relieves students of the burden of figuring out why a word is spelled a certain way. They are free to analyze words and identify patterns on their own. Their brains can then visualize words in context, retrieve that visual image from memory, and create their own associations to help them spell words correctly.

ꕤ Chunking

Chunking is the process of locating and marking specific letter patterns within the passage.

- The six different letter patterns, or chunks, are each assigned a different color. Using color is fun and powerful and creates a strong visual connection to each pattern. The same colors are used throughout all skill development levels of Spelling You See.

- Students will mark the chunks in the passage that are specified in the instructions on the Student Workbook pages. Be certain to check every day to see which letter patterns are being chunked, as they will change from lesson to lesson or even from page to page.

- Close examination of letter patterns and consistent chunking of passages help students to create pictures in their minds of the correct spellings of words.

- Repeated chunking of a familiar passage further establishes a visual memory for irregularly-spelled words and strengthens automatic recall of correct spelling.

- Your student does not need to memorize the lists of chunks, as they are provided on the Student Workbook pages to reference as needed.

- A quick guide to the chunks and their assigned colors can be found on the next page. This can also be downloaded from the Digital Tools on the website.

- Detailed information on each kind of chunk can be found in the lessons in which they are introduced.

- If errors are made (e.g., the student marks something that is not a chunk), the error should be erased and corrected as soon as it is noticed. Ask them to look at the chunk reference box or the page header to see if the letters they marked are listed as a chunk. If a letter pattern is not indicated as a chunk, it should not be marked.

Vowel Chunks (*yellow*) Two or more letters that make a single vowel sound.	aa ae ai ao au aw ay ea ee ei eo eu ew ey eau ia ie ii io iu oa oe oi oo ou ow oy ua ue ui uo uu uy
Bossy *r* Chunks (*purple*) Sometimes called **r-controlled** vowels, the **r** "bosses" the vowel it follows.	ar er ir or ur
Consonant Chunks (*blue*) Two or more letters that make a single consonant sound.	ch gh ph sh th wh wr gn kn dg qu ck tch bb cc dd ff gg hh kk ll mm nn pp rr ss tt vv ww zz
Tricky *y* Guy (*green*) Usually found at the end of words but may be in the middle.	Can sound like long e (baby), long i (fly), or short i (bicycle).
Endings (*pink/red*) Added to a base word to change its meaning.	-ed -es -ful -ing -ly
Silent Letters (*orange*) Only mark silent letters that aren't part of a chunk.	e h l b Other letters may occasionally be silent.
When Chunks Overlap	Some words have overlapping chunks. In lessons with multiple chunks, we suggest marking vowel chunks before Bossy *r* chunks, but Bossy *r* chunks before consonant chunks. If your student chooses a different combination of letters than in the answer key, do not mark it wrong. Discuss their choice and point out other possibilities. Your student may find it helpful to chunk the letter combination that they think will be the most difficult to remember.

✎ Copywork

On Worksheets A–C, students are asked to copy a short selection from the weekly passage.

- English has grown from many different languages and retained inconsistent phonics rules. Copying a familiar passage helps students learn to link how a word sounds to how it looks and is spelled.

- This program emphasizes the development of visual memory, but kinesthetic memory (or muscle memory) is another important part of learning to spell. Recopying the passage leads to familiarity with common letter patterns, as well as with non-phonetic words that are often difficult for students to learn. When copying, students must pay close attention to details in print that might otherwise elude them.

- Studying words within the meaningful context of the passages can help with not only imprinting correct spellings into long-term memory but also retrieving them again. Copywork acts as a cognitive structuring device, sorting information visually so it is more easily organized and processed by the brain.

- If a mistake is made in copywork, students should erase and correct it as soon as it is noticed.

A Note on Handwriting

Students should print their copywork by hand, using pencil so they can correct any errors as soon as they are made. Even if students know and are comfortable using cursive, copywork and dictation should be printed. The goal is to create a visual connection with printed words in the books they read. As far as neatness, as long as your student is able to read back to you what they have written, the quality of their handwriting is not important. Our brains can't fully focus on two things at one time. If neatness is overemphasized, focus is taken away from creating visual memory of correct spelling. The act of forming the letters is the part that leads to muscle memory, regardless of neatness or beauty. Save penmanship practice for another time.

✨ No Rule Day

No Rule Day is an opportunity to develop your student's interest in writing, listening, storytelling, and illustrating; all of which are important components of communication and language development. In part D of each lesson, your student has an opportunity for creative self-expression. Students at this age may have limited writing skills, but they often have unlimited imaginations. No Rule Day offers a chance for their imaginations to soar as they write, dictate, illustrate, or otherwise interpret their ideas.

- The goal is to encourage the free expression of ideas and imagination in a fun way. Don't require more than 10 minutes for this activity unless your student wants to continue.

- Resist the urge to correct handwriting and spelling for the No Rule Day activity. Creating is a different cognitive process than reading, spelling, or copywork. Giving your student an opportunity to create is an important part of their becoming comfortable and adept with their use of language. Focusing too much on spelling or penmanship can stifle the creative process. Your student is more likely to enjoy the writing experience while becoming comfortable with the process if there really are "no rules."

Need Ideas? Here are some to get started:

- Draw something related to the weekly passage. Focus on the animal or its environment and describe it in more detail.

- Write one sentence about the weekly passage.

- Dictate a story to the instructor. Then illustrate it, read it aloud, or use the story as copywork.

- Choose one word or phrase in the passage and illustrate it. Use markers, colored pencils, glitter, a stencil, or other art materials.

- Describe another animal or a pet. How is this animal similar to the one in the passage? How are they different? What would happen if the pet met the animal from the passage? What would the results be if the two animals were crossed into one animal?

🔊 Dictation

On the last day of a *Wild Tales* lesson after shared reading and chunking the passage, students are ready for dictation. Read the story from the lesson instructions, one word at a time, providing all punctuation and capitalization. Detailed instructions are found in Lesson 1.

Dictation Best Practices

- Students should be as relaxed and engaged as possible. Approach dication as a game or a challenge, never as a test. It is simply an opportunity to demonstrate what they have learned so far.

- Tell your student that you will provide all capitalization and punctuation necessary and help with difficult words; remind them that they can ask for help whenever they need it.

- Explain to your student that their paper is "sloppy copy" and that they do not need to erase, unlike in their copywork. Sometimes your student will need to write words several ways before pinpointing the one that "looks right" (their visual memory in action), so it is important to let them compare different spellings. Encourage this by saying, "Try it with and without an *e* at the end. Which one looks right?" Have them draw a line through the wrong word and keep going.

- If they do not come up with the correct spelling themselves and are beginning to get frustrated, write a couple of options yourself on a separate piece of paper. Say, "Here are a couple of options: *wen* or *when*. Which looks right?" Then have them copy the correct spelling. Count their correct choice as a correct word when totaling the number of words spelled correctly.

- Dictation will get easier and faster with more words written correctly as the process becomes more familiar. It is better to spell a few words correctly than to write many words with misspellings!

- Be positive and always count the number of words spelled correctly, not the number spelled incorrectly. If you help your student come up with the correct spelling, count that as a word spelled correctly.

- Watch the Passage Dictation video in the Digital Tools area of the website to see an example of a dictation session.

Once students begin to grasp spelling patterns, reading becomes easier as well. The brain starts to identify patterns within new words through context. Rather than using rote memorization or constantly trying to figure out which rule applies, students simply need to ask themselves, "What did that word that I copied all week look like?" Over time, the brain starts to remember the letter patterns and connect the words in the lesson with other words having the same patterns. Eventually students will link *rain* to *said* as they make the visual connection.

Getting Started   Tips for Success

Here are some tips to help you provide the best experience and to help your student achieve the most spelling success.

Daily Worksheets

Each worksheet has a student checklist for that day's activities. While you will quickly fall into the weekly flow of *Wild Tales*, be sure to review the lesson instructions each day, as weekly lessons and daily worksheets may focus on different letter patterns and activities. Lesson-by-lesson instructions begin on the next page.

Short Lessons

Keep the lessons short and upbeat, offering your student as much help as needed to ensure success. Take the time to read through how the activities should be completed. Descriptions of the five core activities are found in About the Activities beginning on page 5. The activities are not difficult, but they are most effective if they are implemented correctly and consistently.

Instructor's Handbook

Lesson-specific instruction and tips are included in this Handbook for each lesson. These include suggestions about how to handle potentially confusing words or situations. It is a good idea to refer to the Handbook each day until you are familiar with the flow of a lesson. Student Workbook pages include a reminder to check the Handbook whenever there is something new or unusual.

Timers Matter

If a suggested time is given for an activity, set a timer and stick to it even if the activity is not completed. Prioritize sticking with the time limit over completing an entire page of copywork or dictation. Nothing will be gained from soldiering on once a student's attention and stamina have worn thin. Once you and your student have the weekly and daily patterns of activities down, lessons will become easier and faster.

Take Your Time

Be prepared to move a little more slowly at first. You will soon become familiar with the pattern of the daily activities.

Keep Moving

If you don't complete a lesson in a week, don't worry! Just move on to the next one. There is no requirement to finish every page of a lesson. Common words and letter patterns will be repeated many times throughout the course.

Neatness Doesn't Count (Much)

Our brains can only focus on one thing at a time. As long as your student is able to read back to you what they have written and chunk their work, don't be concerned about neatness. Save handwriting instruction for another time.

Please Print

Wild Tales copywork and dictation should be printed, even if your student knows cursive. See A Note on Handwriting on page 8.

Watch and Learn

Videos demonstrating several of the unique activities in the Spelling You See program can be found on the website.

Lesson 1 Vowel Chunks

Before You Begin

If you have not looked over *A Wild Tales Week* and *About the Activities* beginning on page 4, please do so before diving into Lesson 1. Weekly and daily activities repeat each week, so you will find a rhythm as you become comfortable with the program. The first few lessons have very detailed instructions to help you find that rhythm.

	1A	1B	1C	1D	1E
📖 Shared Reading	✓	✓	✓	✓	✓
💬 Chunking					
✏️ Copywork	⏱ 10 min	⏱ 10 min	⏱ 10 min		
✨ No Rule Day				✓	
🔊 Dictation					⏱ 10 min

New This Week: Vowel Chunks

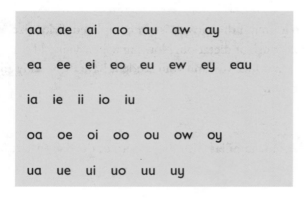

aa ae ai ao au aw ay

ea ee ei eo eu ew ey eau

ia ie ii io iu

oa oe oi oo ou ow oy

ua ue ui uo uu uy

- The first letter pattern you will focus on with your student is vowel chunks. Vowel chunks are usually the most significant source of confusion with spelling, because vowel sounds can be made by a variety of chunks—and vowel chunks can make a variety of sounds.

- The vowels are *a, e, i, o,* and *u*. Sometimes the letters *w* and *y* can act like vowels, so they are also included in some of the vowel chunks. Every syllable has a vowel sound.

- This list of chunks will also be found on the Student Workbook pages. There's no need to memorize them.

- A vowel chunk is composed of two vowels that usually make one sound in a word. Examples are *ea*, *oo*, and *ou*. Focusing on letter patterns in the context of a passage helps a student learn the irregular sounds of the English language.

- Vowel chunks are always marked with yellow in Spelling You See.

- Even if each vowel sound can be heard separately in a vowel pair, as in *radio* or *area*, the pair should still be marked as a vowel chunk unless otherwise noted in the instructions for specific lessons.

- Notice that the three-letter combination *eau* is included in this list. If found, these three letters should be marked as one chunk.

- In words such as *doing* and *being*, we suggest marking the endings rather than vowel chunks when the student is looking for both patterns. Always allow your student to mark the chunks they find most helpful to them.

Lesson 1   Vowel Chunks

📖 Shared Reading

Read the passage aloud to your student, then ask them to read it back to you. Do this regardless of your student's reading level. The purpose is to have the student listen and read the passage exactly as written.

💬 Chunking

Chunk the passage. This means it's time to get out the colored pencils!
Use the color-keyed solutions below to make sure the chunking is complete.

Some sheep are wild. Bighorn sheep live on mountains and high hills. Male sheep are called rams. The bighorn rams have huge horns. They use their horns to fight each other. Flocks of sheep eat grass in the meadows. They climb steep hills to find more food.

vowel chunks: 15

✏️ Copywork

⏱ Set a timer and always allow the student to stop after 10 minutes, even if they have not copied the entire selection.

If they make a mistake, they should erase the incorrect word as soon as it is spotted and rewrite the word correctly.

After time is up, have your student chunk their work, looking at the opposite page as needed. Don't be tempted to skip this part, because paying close attention to their own writing in order to mark it will help further establish the letter patterns in their memory.

✨ No Rule Day

For this activity, don't correct spelling or handwriting. While it's important to make prompt corrections in copywork and dicatation exercises, using "invented spelling" for this activity won't affect a student's long-term spelling success. Until your student's spelling mastery becomes automatic, trying to recall correct spelling can stifle the creative process.

This activity is meant to be fun, so don't require more than ten minutes unless your student wants to keep working.

🔊 Dictation

📖 Read About the Activities: Dictation on page 10 before your first dictation session.

⏱ Set the timer for ten minutes. When the timer goes off, stop, even if the whole passage is not complete. Count the number of words written, even those where the student asked for help. The goal is quality, not quantity.

Read the passage aloud one word at a time until your student needs help with a word. Provide all capitalization and punctuation as you go. Go as slowly or as quickly as they need. Stop to help but do not stop the clock.

Address misspellings as they occur. Suggestions on how to do this are in About the Activities: Dictation on page 10.

Some sheep are wild. Bighorn sheep live on mountains and high hills. Male sheep are called rams. The bighorn rams have huge horns. They use their horns to fight each other. Flocks of sheep eat grass in the meadows. They climb steep hills to find more food.

Word Count: 47

Lesson 2 More Vowel Chunks

	2A	2B	2C	2D	2E
📖 Shared Reading	✓	✓	✓	✓	✓
💬 Chunking					
✏️ Copywork	⏱ 10 min	⏱ 10 min	⏱ 10 min		
✨ No Rule Day				✓	
🔊 Dictation					⏱ 10 min

📖 Shared Reading

Read the passage aloud to each other, as described in About the Activities: Shared Reading on page 5.

⚠ Don't be tempted to skip this activity, regardless of your student's reading level! Listening, reading, and spelling are very different skills, but they work together to strengthen overall language development.

Your student should follow along with their finger, pointing to each word as you read the passage aloud. Pointing to each word as they hear it helps students focus on beginning letters, make connections between sounds and letter patterns, and practice left-to-right eye movement.

Lesson 2 More Vowel Chunks

💬 Chunking

For this lesson, your student will need to chunk:

vowel chunks

Remind your student that they can use the reference boxes on their Student Workbook pages to help them find all of the chunks. They don't need to try to memorize them!

Be patient and work with your student as they become familiar with the chunking process. They are learning to look closely and notice patterns in printed language. It will become easier with experience.

If your student doesn't find all of the chunks on their first try, help them by telling them how many more chunks they need to find or showing them the line where the missing chunk can be found or the word that contains it.

Bald eagles fly high in the air. The eagle has special eyes. It can see to the front and the side at the same time. It can see a fish from high in the air. The eagle dives into the water and catches the fish in its claws. A fish makes a good meal.

vowel chunks: 12

🔊 Dictation

⏱ Remember to limit the time spent on dictation to 10 minutes.

Don't worry if a passage is not finished during that time. Your student will have many opportunities to practice the words in other contexts.

Bald eagles fly high in the air. The eagle has special eyes. It can see to the front and the side at the same time. It can see a fish from high in the air. The eagle dives into the water and catches the fish in its claws. A fish makes a good meal.

Word Count: 54

Lesson 3   Consonant Chunks

	3A	3B	3C	3D	3E
📖 Shared Reading	✓	✓	✓	✓	✓
💬 Chunking					
✏️ Copywork	⏱ 10 min	⏱ 10 min	⏱ 10 min		
✨ No Rule Day				✓	
🔊 Dictation					⏱ 10 min

New This Week: Consonant Chunks

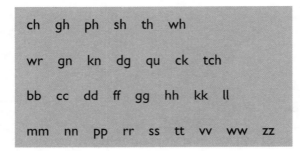

ch	gh	ph	sh	th	wh
wr	gn	kn	dg	qu	ck	tch
bb	cc	dd	ff	gg	hh	kk	ll
mm	nn	pp	rr	ss	tt	vv	ww	zz

- The consonants consist of all the letters that are not vowels. A consonant chunk is made up of two consonants that make one sound in a word, such as *th* or *kn*.

- There is a complete list of consonant chunks on the student's workbook pages, so there is no need to memorize the chunks.

- Take your time as your student becomes familiar with these new letter patterns. Offer as much help as is needed.

- Explain to your student that while some consonant chunks make the sounds that you might expect, some change their sounds completely when they appear in a chunk, and some are even silent! Don't spend a lot of time discussing or emphasizing rules; your student will learn the correct spelling patterns by practicing with the chunks.

- Blends are not included with the consonant chunks. In a blend, each letter can be heard making its expected sound. The *st* in *stop* is an example of a blend.

- Consonant chunks are always marked with blue in Spelling You See.

Lesson 3 Consonant Chunks

📖 Shared Reading

Read the passage aloud as your student follows along, then have your student read it back to you.

🗩 Chunking

For this lesson, your student will need to chunk:

consonant chunks

Bullfrogs like ponds and marshy places. They eat fish and other small animals. A bullfrog's mouth is big enough to swallow lunch whole. The male bullfrog has a very loud call. The sound can be heard day and night.

consonant chunks: 17

✏️ Copywork

Your student should always chunk the section of the passage that they have written for copywork. Paying close attention to their own writing in order to mark it will help further establish the letter patterns in their memory. They can look back at the previous page at the consonant chunk box if they need help finding chunks.

✨ No Rule Day

Be sure to make No Rule Day fun and relaxed. See page 9 for ideas.

🕙 Your student shouldn't work for more than 10 minutes on this activity unless they would like to continue.

🔊 Dictation

🕙 Remember to limit the time spent on dictation to 10 minutes.

Don't worry if a passage is not finished during that time. Your student will have many opportunities to practice the words in other contexts.

Bullfrogs like ponds and marshy places. They eat fish and other small animals. A bullfrog's mouth is big enough to swallow lunch whole. The male bullfrog has a very loud call. The sound can be heard day and night.

Word Count: 39

	4A	4B	4C	4D	4E
📖 Shared Reading	✓	✓	✓	✓	✓
💬 Chunking	▬	▬	▬	▬	▬
✏️ Copywork	⏱ 10 min	⏱ 10 min	⏱ 10 min		
🪄 No Rule Day				✓	
🔊 Dictation					⏱ 10 min

Lesson 4 More Consonant Chunks

🗨 Chunking

For this lesson, your student will need to chunk:

consonant chunks

If chunks are missed, tell the student how many more they are looking for ("There is one more consonant chunk. Can you find it?"). Remind them that they can use the colored reference boxes to check if they are unsure whether certain letters make up a chunk.

A giraffe is very tall. It has a long neck. It eats leaves from high tree branches. It eats a lot! The giraffe's spotted coat makes it hard to see in the bushes. Some giraffes fight by hitting their necks and heads together. Ouch!

consonant chunks: 17

✏ Copywork

Continue having your student complete ten minutes of copywork and then chunking what they have written as established in previous lessons. This is the way copywork should be completed throughout the *Wild Tales* program.

🔊 Dictation

⏱ Remember to limit the time spent on dictation to 10 minutes.

Don't worry if a passage is not finished during that time. Your student will have many opportunities to practice the words in other contexts.

A giraffe is very tall. It has a long neck. It eats leaves from high tree branches. It eats a lot! The giraffe's spotted coat makes it hard to see in the bushes. Some giraffes fight by hitting their necks and heads together. Ouch!

Word Count: 44

Lesson 5 Bossy r Chunks

	5A	5B	5C	5D	5E
📖 Shared Reading	✓	✓	✓	✓	✓
💬 Chunking	▨	▨	▨	▨	▨
✏️ Copywork	⏱ 10 min	⏱ 10 min	⏱ 10 min		
✨ No Rule Day				✓	
🔊 Dictation					⏱ 10 min

New This Week: Bossy r Chunks

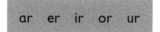

- When a vowel (*a, e, i, o, u*) is followed by an *r*, the vowel sound changes. The *r* "bosses" the vowel.

- Notice how the *r* changes the sound of the vowel in the following word pairs: *cat–car, bed–her, sit–sir, hot–for, pup–purr*. Point out how the vowel makes its regular short sound in the first word, but changes in the second word as it is affected by the *r*. Because the *r* controls the sound of the vowel, we call it a "Bossy" *r*.

- It is especially difficult to distinguish between *er*, *ir*, and *ur* sounds when hearing them. That is why it is so important to create a visual memory of the spelling of words that include these sounds. For example, there is no way to spell the word *bird* without knowing the proper pattern.

- There are some words (*board, their, your*) that have a vowel chunk followed by a Bossy *r* chunk. If a student is marking both vowel chunks and Bossy *r* chunks in a lesson, we suggest marking the vowel chunk first because vowel chunks are the most common stumbling block to correct spelling. (Always allow your student to choose and mark the chunk they feel will be most helpful to them.)

- If there is a Bossy *r* chunk overlapping a consonant chunk (*stirrup, hurry*), we suggest marking the Bossy *r* chunk. Because the vowel sound before the Bossy *r* often sounds the same regardless of which vowel is used, students usually find it most helpful to visualize the correct vowel-Bossy *r* chunk rather than the consonant chunk.

- Bossy *r* chunks are always marked with purple in Spelling You See.

Lesson 5 Bossy *r* Chunks

💬 Chunking

For this lesson, your student will need to chunk:

Bossy *r* chunks

The wat**er** b**ear** is not really a b**ear**. It is small**er** than a grain of salt. It lives in wet moss on the b**ar**k of trees. The wat**er** b**ear** has eight legs. A wat**er** b**ear** can s**ur**vive being v**er**y hot or v**er**y cold. It can even s**ur**vive being dried out. Just add wat**er**, and it st**ar**ts moving again.

Bossy *r* chunks: 15

🔊 Dictation

⏱ Remember to limit the time spent on dictation to 10 minutes.

The water bear is not really a bear. It is smaller than a grain of salt. It lives in wet moss on the bark of trees. The water bear has eight legs. A water bear can survive being very hot or very cold. It can even survive being dried out. Just add water, and it starts moving again.

Word Count: 58

Lesson 6   Tricky y Guy

	6A	6B	6C	6D	6E
📖 Shared Reading	✓	✓	✓	✓	✓
💬 Chunking	�	▪	▪	▪	▪
✏️ Copywork	⏱ 10 min	⏱ 10 min	⏱ 10 min		
🪄 No Rule Day				✓	
🔊 Dictation					⏱ 10 min

New This Week: Tricky y Guy

- The letter *y* is usually a consonant (*year, yak*), but sometimes it is "tricky" and sounds like a vowel. Tricky *y* Guy is usually found at the end of words but may be in the middle. It can sound like long *e* (*baby*), long *i* (*fly*), or short *i* (*bicycle*).

- Because this pattern is just one letter, there is no colored reference box on the student workbook pages.

- Tricky *y* Guy is always marked with green in Spelling You See.

💬 Chunking

For this lesson, your student will need to chunk:

Tricky *y* Guy

A firefly is really a beetle. It flies over grassy fields. Each firefly has a tiny light. Together the lights make a pretty sight. The firefly does not like dry places. It likes damp ground.

Tricky y Guy: 8

Lesson 6 Tricky y Guy

✏️ Copywork

⏱ Continue to limit time spent in copywork to 10 minutes each day.

After 10 minutes, have your student chunk the passage they have written, using the left-hand page as a guide if necessary.

🔊 Dictation

⏱ Remember to limit the time spent on dictation to 10 minutes.

A firefly is really a beetle. It flies over grassy fields. Each firefly has a tiny light. Together the lights make a pretty sight. The firefly does not like dry places. It likes damp ground.

Word Count: 35

Lesson 7 Silent Letters

	7A	7B	7C	7D	7E
📖 Shared Reading	✓	✓	✓	✓	✓
🗩 Chunking					
✏️ Copywork	⏱ 10 min	⏱ 10 min	⏱ 10 min		
✨ No Rule Day				✓	
🔊 Dictation					⏱ 10 min

New This Week: Silent Letters

- A word may have silent letters that are not part of chunks. In this lesson, you will find a silent *e* at the end of several words.

- Silent *e* is often found at the end of words. Some words in other lessons may have a silent *b* or *h*. Examples are thum*b* and o*h*. The *l* in words like wa*l*k or cou*l*d is also silent. Notice that sometimes a silent letter changes the sound of the vowel, just as Bossy *r* does.

- Silent letters will always be marked in orange in Spelling You See.

- Only silent letters that are not part of other chunks should be marked. This will rule out, for example, the *h* in words like *when*, or one or more of the letters in many vowel chunks. For this reason, silent letters are the last ones to be marked when marking multiple chunks in a passage.

- If your student chooses to mark silent letters that are part of another chunk, do not mark them incorrect. Instead, take the opportunity to discuss the other letter patterns found in the word.

- Because this pattern is just one letter, a colored reference box is not provided on the Student Workbook pages.

Lesson 7 Silent Letters

℘ Chunking

For this lesson, your student will need to chunk:

silent letters

Some geese live on farms. Canada geese are wild. Many geese flying together make the shape of the letter *V*. Huge flocks of them rest in parks. They like to feed on large lawns. The geese make a lot of noise!

silent letters: 14

◁ⁱⁱ) Dictation

⏱ Remember to limit the time spent on dictation to 10 minutes.

Move on to a new lesson the next day, even if the passage or lesson is not completed.

When guiding dictation, do not tell the student to "sound out" a word. Instead, remind them of another word that has the same letter combination or simply tell them the troublesome letters.

Some geese live on farms. Canada geese are wild. Many geese flying together make the shape of the letter *V*. Huge flocks of them rest in parks. They like to feed on large lawns. The geese make a lot of noise!

Word Count: 41

Lesson 8   Vowel Chunks

	8A	8B	8C	8D	8E
📖 Shared Reading	✓	✓	✓	✓	✓
💬 Chunking					
✏️ Copywork	⏱ 10 min	⏱ 10 min	⏱ 10 min		
🪄 No Rule Day				✓	
🔊 Dictation					⏱ 10 min

Lesson 8   Vowel Chunks

🗩 Chunking

For this lesson, your student will need to chunk:

vowel chunks

Remember that vowel chunks are two letters together that form a single vowel sound. Many vowel chunks are made up of only vowels—*a, e, i, o,* and *u*—but *w* and *y* can also be part of a vowel chunk, as in *day* or *how*.

A list of vowel chunks can be found on the Student Workbook pages. There is no need to memorize the chunks.

How does a chick hatch out of its shell? It has a tooth at the end of its beak! Using this tooth, it pecks at its shell. The chick pushes while pecking. The push turns the chick inside the shell. The chick pecks a new part of the shell. After a while, the shell breaks. The chick can get out!

vowel chunks: 9

🔊 Dictation

Continue completing dictation as you have learned in previous lessons. You will complete one dictation session in each lesson through the end of the *Wild Tales* program.

How does a chick hatch out of its shell? It has a tooth at the end of its beak! Using this tooth, it pecks at its shell. The chick pushes while pecking. The push turns the chick inside the shell. The chick pecks a new part of the shell. After a while, the shell breaks. The chick can get out!

Word Count: 60

	9A	9B	9C	9D	9E
📖 Shared Reading	✓	✓	✓	✓	✓
🗨 Chunking					
✏ Copywork	⏱ 10 min	⏱ 10 min	⏱ 10 min		
✨ No Rule Day				✓	
🔊 Dictation					⏱ 10 min

New This Week: Multiple Chunks

- Beginning with this lesson, your student will be identifying different letter chunks and patterns each day. The focus of the day's chunking activity is identified in the instructions on the Student Workbook pages.

Lesson 9 Vowel and Consonant Chunks, Silent Letters

🗣 Chunking

For this lesson, your student will need to chunk:

vowel chunks   **consonant chunks**   **silent letters**

A trunk is more than a long nose. An elephant can pull water up its trunk. Then it sprays itself to keep cool. An elephant can grab food with its trunk. It can even use the end of its trunk to pick up very small things!

vowel chunks: 4

A trunk is more than a long nose. An elephant can pull water up its trunk. Then it sprays itself to keep cool. An elephant can grab food with its trunk. It can even use the end of its trunk to pick up very small things!

consonant chunks: 10

A trunk is more than a long nose. An elephant can pull water up its trunk. Then it sprays itself to keep cool. An elephant can grab food with its trunk. It can even use the end of its trunk to pick up very small things!

silent letters: 3

🔊 Dictation

A trunk is more than a long nose. An elephant can pull water up its trunk. Then it sprays itself to keep cool. An elephant can grab food with its trunk. It can even use the end of its trunk to pick up very small things!

Word Count: 46

Lesson 10 Vowel, Bossy *r*, and Consonant Chunks

	10A	10B	10C	10D	10E
📖 Shared Reading	✓	✓	✓	✓	✓
💬 Chunking					
✏️ Copywork	⏱ 10 min	⏱ 10 min	⏱ 10 min		
🪄 No Rule Day				✓	
🔊 Dictation					⏱ 10 min

Lesson 10 Vowel, Bossy *r*, and Consonant Chunks

♀ Chunking

For this lesson, your student will need to chunk:

vowel chunks   **consonant chunks**   **Bossy *r* chunks**

Remind your student that they should use the reference boxes on their Student Workbook pages to help them find all of the chunks. They don't need to try to memorize them! The reference box will remind them which chunks they are looking for each day.

Have you ever seen a hummingbird? It can fly forward and backward. It can stay still in midair by beating its wings very fast. No other bird can fly like this! That is why the hummingbird has to eat a lot of food.

vowel chunks: 7

Have you ever seen a hummingbird? It can fly forward and backward. It can stay still in midair by beating its wings very fast. No other bird can fly like this! That is why the hummingbird has to eat a lot of food.

consonant chunks: 9

Have you ever seen a hummingbird? It can fly forward and backward. It can stay still in midair by beating its wings very fast. No other bird can fly like this! That is why the hummingbird has to eat a lot of food.

Bossy *r* chunks: 10

◁») Dictation

Have you ever seen a hummingbird? It can fly forward and backward. It can stay still in midair by beating its wings very fast. No other bird can fly like this! That is why the hummingbird has to eat a lot of food.

Word Count: 43

	11A	11B	11C	11D	11E
Shared Reading	✓	✓	✓	✓	✓
Chunking					
Copywork	⏱ 10 min	⏱ 10 min	⏱ 10 min		
No Rule Day				✓	
Dictation					⏱ 10 min

Lesson 11   Vowel, Bossy *r*, and Consonant Chunks

⌇ Chunking

For this lesson, your student will need to chunk:

<u>vowel chunks</u>   <u>consonant chunks</u>   <u>Bossy *r* chunks</u>

Notice that the same vowel chunk can make different sounds. Point out that the *ow* in *shows* sounds different from the same vowel chunk in *how*. The chunk *ea* makes a different sound in *bear* than it does in *eat*. These are examples of why spelling English words can be challenging! Take a moment to praise your student for identifying these look-alikes that do not sound alike.

Notice that the three-letter combination *tch* is marked as a consonant chunk. It is one of the few three-letter chunks.

The combination *mb* is not considered a consonant chunk because each letter is part of a different syllable in many English words (*combine, steamboat*). If your student marks it as a consonant chunk, it is not wrong, but take time to share this information with them.

A mother black bear helps her cubs find food. She shows them how to look under rocks for bugs. The cubs learn how to catch fish and dig for mice. She shows them where to look for berries and nuts. They will also eat a honeycomb with the bees still on it!

vowel chunks: 14

A mother black bear helps her cubs find food. She shows them how to look under rocks for bugs. The cubs learn how to catch fish and dig for mice. She shows them where to look for berries and nuts. They will also eat a honeycomb with the bees still on it!

consonant chunks: 19

A mother black bear helps her cubs find food. She shows them how to look under rocks for bugs. The cubs learn how to catch fish and dig for mice. She shows them where to look for berries and nuts. They will also eat a honeycomb with the bees still on it!

Bossy *r* chunks: 10

◁)) Dictation

A mother black bear helps her cubs find food. She shows them how to look under rocks for bugs. The cubs learn how to catch fish and dig for mice. She shows them where to look for berries and nuts. They will also eat a honeycomb with the bees still on it!

Word Count: 52

Lesson 12   Vowel and Consonant Chunks, Silent Letters

	12A	12B	12C	12D	12E
📖 Shared Reading	✓	✓	✓	✓	✓
💬 Chunking					
✏️ Copywork	⏱ 10 min	⏱ 10 min	⏱ 10 min		
🪄 No Rule Day				✓	
🔊 Dictation					⏱ 10 min

💬 Chunking

For this lesson, your student will need to chunk:

vowel chunks   **consonant chunks**   **silent letters**

While *e* is the most common silent letter in English, other letters can be silent too. Notice that the *l* in *walking* changes the sound of the *a*. Silent letters may not make a sound themselves, but they definitely have an impact on how words are pronounced.

There is an insect called a walking stick. What do you think it looks like? Yes, it looks like a stick with legs. When it stays still, it looks like a branch. A hungry bird looking for an insect to eat can't find the walking stick!

vowel chunks: 7

There is an insect called a walking stick. What do you think it looks like? Yes, it looks like a stick with legs. When it stays still, it looks like a branch. A hungry bird looking for an insect to eat can't find the walking stick!

consonant chunks: 12

There is an insect called a walking stick. What do you think it looks like? Yes, it looks like a stick with legs. When it stays still, it looks like a branch. A hungry bird looking for an insect to eat can't find the walking stick!

silent letters: 6

🔊 Dictation

There is an insect called a walking stick. What do you think it looks like? Yes, it looks like a stick with legs. When it stays still, it looks like a branch. A hungry bird looking for an insect to eat can't find the walking stick!

Word Count: 46

Suggested Order for Chunking

In Lesson 13, your student will begin marking more than one kind of chunk each day. The recommended order when marking more than one kind of chunk in a passage is determined by the letter patterns most commonly involved in misspellings. These are patterns that are most likely to trip up a student when they are trying to correctly spell a word. Students should make multiple passes through the passage to mark different kinds of chunks rather than attempting to find all of them at once.

Suggested Order for Chunking

<u>vowel chunks</u>

<u>Bossy *r* chunks</u>

<u>consonant chunks</u>

<u>Tricky *y* Guy</u>

<u>endings</u>

<u>silent letters</u>

The purpose of chunking is to train the student to look carefully at letter patterns and create a mental picture of the correct spelling. **If they choose to chunk a different letter pattern than is indicated in the answer key, it is not necessarily wrong.** Discuss their choice and point out other possibilities. Your student should chunk the letter combination that they think will be the most difficult for them to remember. The provided solutions will reflect the stated focus of the lesson and follow our suggested order. If your student chooses to chunk a different letter pattern (such as marking the *rr* rather than the *ur* in *hurries*), be certain to adjust the total chunks when checking their work. See the next section for information on what to do when chunks overlap.

Overlapping Chunks

Look at the word *beard*. It has a vowel chunk (*ea*) that overlaps with a Bossy *r* chunk (*ar*); the letter *a* is part of both chunks. If the lesson's focus is only vowel chunks or only Bossy *r* chunks, this is not an issue. However, as your student advances through *Wild Tales*, they will begin to mark multiple kinds of chunks in a passage and they may need to choose which they are going to mark. Marking chunks on top of one another in different colors would only cause confusion. When faced with overlapping chunks, discuss which pattern your student believes will be more difficult for them to remember and mark that one.

Avoiding Chunking Overload

Even though your student may be quite adept at finding all of the specified letter patterns, being asked to find several kinds of chunks in one sitting could get time-consuming and stressful for them. Spending more than 10 minutes identifying the different chunks in a passage could make spelling into a burden, causing learning to shut down. If this is regularly happening, have a conversation with your student and identify two or three kinds of chunks that they feel would be the most helpful for them to mark. Another option would be to focus on one type of chunk each day during the week.

Lesson 13   Bossy *r* and Consonant Chunks, Silent Letters

	13A	13B	13C	13D	13E
📖 Shared Reading	✓	✓	✓	✓	✓
💬 Chunking					
✏️ Copywork	⏱ 10 min	⏱ 10 min	⏱ 10 min		
✨ No Rule Day				✓	
🔊 Dictation					⏱ 10 min

💬 Chunking

For this lesson, your student will need to chunk:

Bossy *r* chunks   **consonant chunks**   **silent letters**

In this lesson, your student will begin to mark more than one kind of chunk each day. Remember that chunks may overlap (see page 35). We recommend marking Bossy *r* chunks before consonant chunks, and the solutions provided here reflect that. However, if your student marks the *rr* chunk in *carry* rather than the *ar* chunk, they are not wrong! The purpose of chunking is to train the mind to look carefully at how words are spelled. This is a good opportunity to discuss which letter combination your student thinks will be most difficult to remember. That is the chunk they should then mark. Rather than attempting to mark all chunks in one pass through the passage, students should mark all of one kind of chunk, then make another pass to mark the next kind, and so on.

Camels are called "ships of the desert." Like big ships, camels carry loads from place to place. Camels have big feet that spread as they walk. That way they don't sink in the sand! Camels are a good way to travel in the desert.

Bossy *r* chunks: 5   consonant chunks: 10   silent letters: 7

🔊 Dictation

Camels are called "ships of the desert." Like big ships, camels carry loads from place to place. Camels have big feet that spread as they walk. That way they don't sink in the sand! Camels are a good way to travel in the desert.

Word Count: 44

	14A	14B	14C	14D	14E
📖 Shared Reading	✓	✓	✓	✓	✓
💬 Chunking					
✏️ Copywork	⏱ 10 min	⏱ 10 min	⏱ 10 min		
✨ No Rule Day				✓	
🔊 Dictation					⏱ 10 min

💬 Chunking

For this lesson, your student will need to chunk:

Bossy *r* chunks   **consonant chunks**   **Tricky *y* Guy**

You may wonder why, if there are overlapping chunks in a word (such as *hurries* in this week's passage), we recommend chunking the Bossy *r* chunks before the consonant chunks. Read the following pairs aloud and listen to how the vowel is changed by the *r* following it: *had* and *hard*; *fen* and *fern*; *bid* and *bird*; *tot* and *tort*; *hut* and *hurt*. In fact, *er*, *ir*, and *ur* all make the same sound in these examples. By looking for and marking Bossy *r* chunks, students are creating visual memory for the proper spelling of these words that cannot be spelled phonetically.

If your student prefers to mark consonant chunks rather than the recommended Bossy *r* chunks when they overlap, that is fine. Talk about their choice and ask them which chunk will help them the most to remember the correct spelling. Remember to adjust the total number of each type of chunk when checking their work against the solutions in this Handbook.

Why doesn't a spider stick to its own web? The spider weaves its web in a special way. Some parts of the web are sticky. Bugs get stuck there. The spider hurries along the parts of the web that aren't sticky. Then the spider gets the bugs!

Bossy *r* chunks: 10   consonant chunks: 15   Tricky *y* Guy: 3

🔊 Dictation

Why doesn't a spider stick to its own web? The spider weaves its web in a special way. Some parts of the web are sticky. Bugs get stuck there. The spider hurries along the parts of the web that aren't sticky. Then the spider gets the bugs!

Word Count: 47

Lesson 15   Vowel and Consonant Chunks

	15A	15B	15C	15D	15E
📖 Shared Reading	✓	✓	✓	✓	✓
💬 Chunking					
✏️ Copywork	⏱ 10 min	⏱ 10 min	⏱ 10 min		
✨ No Rule Day				✓	
🔊 Dictation					⏱ 10 min

💬 Chunking

For this lesson, your student will need to chunk:

<u>vowel chunks</u>   <u>consonant chunks</u>

What is the biggest animal in the world? It's the blue whale. A blue whale weighs three tons when it is born. That's about the same as three small cars! A baby blue whale drinks more than 100 gallons of milk a day. What a large baby!

<u>vowel chunks</u>: 8   <u>consonant chunks</u>: 18

🔊 Dictation

What is the biggest animal in the world? It's the blue whale. A blue whale weighs three tons when it is born. That's about the same as three small cars! A baby blue whale drinks more than 100 gallons of milk a day. What a large baby!

Word Count: 47

Lesson 16 Vowel, Bossy *r*, and Consonant Chunks

	16A	16B	16C	16D	16E
📖 Shared Reading	✓	✓	✓	✓	✓
💬 Chunking					
✏️ Copywork	⏱ 10 min	⏱ 10 min	⏱ 10 min		
✨ No Rule Day				✓	
🔊 Dictation					⏱ 10 min

💬 Chunking

For this lesson, your student will need to chunk:

vowel chunks   **Bossy *r* chunks**   consonant chunks

Discuss the vowel chunk *ea*. Notice the sound it makes in the word *each* and compare it to the sound it makes in *bear*. Which sound does it make in *near*? Maybe not the one you expect! *Bear* and *near* do not rhyme, even though it appears that they should. If you were to pronounce *bear* so it rhymes with *near*, it would sound like a very different word that already exists (*beer*).

Musk oxen live in the cold north. They have woolly coats. Each ox has two sharp horns. If a wolf pack or a bear comes near, the adult musk oxen form a circle. They keep the young oxen safe in the middle of the circle.

vowel chunks: 9   Bossy *r* chunks: 7   consonant chunks: 13

🔊 Dictation

Musk oxen live in the cold north. They have woolly coats. Each ox has two sharp horns. If a wolf pack or a bear comes near, the adult musk oxen form a circle. They keep the young oxen safe in the middle of the circle.

Word Count: 45

	17A	17B	17C	17D	17E
📖 Shared Reading	✓	✓	✓	✓	✓
🗨 Chunking					
✏ Copywork	⏱ 10 min	⏱ 10 min	⏱ 10 min		
🪄 No Rule Day				✓	
🔊 Dictation					⏱ 10 min

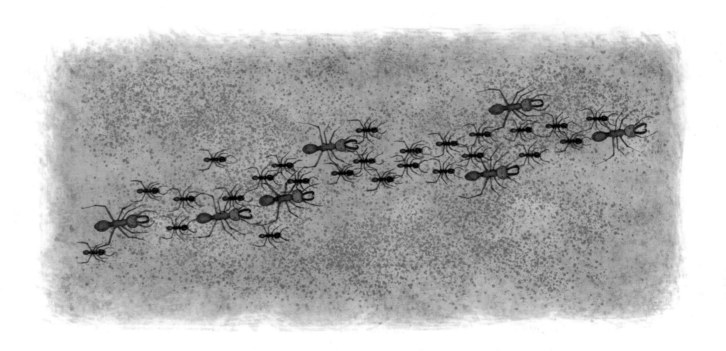

Lesson 17   Vowel, Bossy *r*, and Consonant Chunks; Silent Letters

ᗏ Chunking

For this lesson, your student will need to chunk:

<u>vowel chunks</u>   <u>**Bossy *r* chunks**</u>   <u>consonant chunks</u>   <u>silent letters</u>

For this lesson, your student will be asked to mark four of the different chunks they have been studying. Stop and congratulate your student on how many letter patterns they can identify! If marking multiple chunks is overwhelming to your student, see Avoiding Chunking Overload on page 35 for suggestions.

Not all ants live in the ground. Some army ants move together in a large group. When they stop, they make a nest with their bodies. Many worker ants hook their legs together to make outer and inner walls. Other workers work in the rooms formed by the living walls.

vowel chunks: 10   <u>Bossy *r* chunks: 13</u>   consonant chunks: 16   silent letters: 6

◁ᵢᵢ Dictation

Not all ants live in the ground. Some army ants move together in a large group. When they stop, they make a nest with their bodies. Many worker ants hook their legs together to make outer and inner walls. Other workers work in the rooms formed by the living walls.

Word Count: 50

Lesson 18 Vowel, Bossy *r*, and Consonant Chunks; Endings

	18A	18B	18C	18D	18E
📖 Shared Reading	✓	✓	✓	✓	✓
💬 Chunking					
✏️ Copywork	⏱ 10 min	⏱ 10 min	⏱ 10 min		
✨ No Rule Day				✓	
🔊 Dictation					⏱ 10 min

New This Week: Endings

-ed -es -ful -ing -ly

- Endings are added to a base word to change the meaning or the part of speech. Endings are quite powerful; they can make a verb into a noun, a noun into an adjective, or an adjective into an adverb! They can even make a single noun plural. You do not need to worry about parts of speech at this point; simply mark the endings in red or pink. A list of endings to look for is provided on the student worksheet.

- If the student marks *-ly* as an ending in a word like *only*, do not mark it wrong, even though it is not technically an ending added to a base word. Base words and endings are not a part of the skill development stage covered in *Wild Tales* and other levels of Spelling You See. They are covered in the next stage, word extension, introduced in *Ancient Achievements* and the focus of *Modern Milestones*. For more information on the developmental stages of spelling, visit spellingyousee.com.

- The *est* and *en* letter combinations frequently appear as part of a base word (*west*, *ten*). They have not been listed as endings in this level.

- In words such as *doing* and *being*, we suggest marking the endings rather than vowel chunks when the student is looking for both patterns. Allow your student to mark the chunk they find most helpful to them.

Lesson 18 Vowel, Bossy *r*, and Consonant Chunks; Endings

📖 Shared Reading

The word *splash* is an example of *onomatopoeia* (pronounced *on-uh-maht-uh-PEE-uh*). That's a fun word to say that means *fun words to say*! More precisely, it means words that look like and are spelled like the sounds they represent. Some examples are *thump*, *sizzle*, and *boing*. Onomatopoeia is used for lots of animal sounds, too: *oink*, *meow*, and *buzz* are all examples. Can you and your student think of any onomatopoeia that animals in the passages might say?

💬 Chunking

For this lesson, your student will need to chunk:

<u>vowel chunks</u>   <u>**Bossy *r* chunks**</u>   <u>consonant chunks</u>   <u>endings</u>

A mother sea turtle swims along. At last she crawls up on the same sandy beach where she hatched long ago. After digging a hole in the sand, she lays her eggs. She covers the eggs with sand. Slowly she heads back into the sea. Splash!

vowel chunks: 7   Bossy *r* chunks: 6   consonant chunks: 19   endings: 3

🔊 Dictation

A mother sea turtle swims along. At last she crawls up on the same sandy beach where she hatched long ago. After digging a hole in the sand, she lays her eggs. She covers the eggs with sand. Slowly she heads back into the sea. Splash!

Word Count: 46

Pause and Reflect

Lesson 18 is the last lesson of Part 1 of the Student Workbook. This is a great time to pause and evaluate how the program is working for you and your student. Here are some questions that can help you assess how your student's spelling skills are progressing.

- Has dictation accuracy increased? A gradual increase in the number of words spelled correctly indicates a developing confidence in spelling.

- Has the speed of dictation increased (e.g., more words correctly spelled in a shorter period of time)? Although time is not tracked in the dictation exercise, you should see the number of words spelled correctly increasing, indicating that more words are being written correctly in a shorter time. You may find that your student is completing the entire passage before the ten-minute time limit is up.

- Have you seen a transfer of spelling skills into writing for other subjects? Frequently-used words are often not spelled phonetically, so spelling these words correctly is a strong indication that correct spelling is being written into long-term memory.

	19A	19B	19C	19D	19E
📖 Shared Reading	✓	✓	✓	✓	✓
💬 Chunking					
✏️ Copywork	⏱ 10 min	⏱ 10 min	⏱ 10 min		
✨ No Rule Day				✓	
🔊 Dictation					⏱ 10 min

💬 Chunking

For this lesson, your student will need to chunk:

vowel chunks

The first lesson of Part 2 reviews vowel chunks. Notice again the different chunks that can make the same sound. In the passage, *people*, *clean*, and *needs* all have the same sound but different vowel chunks. Sometimes the same chunk will make different sounds in different words, as in *ocean* and *eat*. Vowel chunks often create the most confusion in spelling, so it is good to pay close attention to how they are used.

Some people use sponges to clean. Did you know that sponges are animals? They live in the ocean. They are attached to rocks or the sea floor. The sponge has holes that let in water. As the water flows through the holes, the sponge gets the food it needs to eat.

vowel chunks: 14

🔊 Dictation

Take a moment to think about your dictation sessions. Review the instructions on page 10 and the online videos to ensure that your student is getting the most from this activity.

Some people use sponges to clean. Did you know that sponges are animals? They live in the ocean. They are attached to rocks or the sea floor. The sponge has holes that let in water. As the water flows through the holes, the sponge gets the food it needs to eat.

Word Count: 51

Lesson 20 Consonant Chunks

	20A	20B	20C	20D	20E
📖 Shared Reading	✓	✓	✓	✓	✓
🗩 Chunking					
✏️ Copywork	⏱ 10 min	⏱ 10 min	⏱ 10 min		
✨ No Rule Day				✓	
🔊 Dictation					⏱ 10 min

🗩 Chunking

For this lesson, your student will need to chunk:

consonant chunks

Remember how consonant chunks differ from blends. In consonant blends, you can hear each letter's individual sound. Conveniently, the word *blend* has two examples of blends: *bl* and *nd*. In consonant chunks, you may hear only the sound of one letter (as in the *ck* in *back*), a new sound (*th* in *sloth*), or even no sound at all (*gh* in *tightly*). In the consonant chunk *qu*, one of the letters is not even a consonant! Given how tricky they can be, consonant chunks are the focus this week.

A sloth spends most of its life upside down. It hangs from a tree branch. The sloth digs its sharp claws into the branch and holds on tightly. The sloth eats leaves from the tree. Then it falls asleep upside down. It is hard to get a sloth to move from its tree!

consonant chunks: 14

🔊 Dictation

A sloth spends most of its life upside down. It hangs from a tree branch. The sloth digs its sharp claws into the branch and holds on tightly. The sloth eats leaves from the tree. Then it falls asleep upside down. It is hard to get a sloth to move from its tree!

Word Count: 53

Lesson 21 Vowel and Consonant Chunks

	21A	21B	21C	21D	21E
🕮 Shared Reading	✓	✓	✓	✓	✓
🗩 Chunking					
✏ Copywork	🕙 10 min	🕙 10 min	🕙 10 min		
🪄 No Rule Day				✓	
🔊 Dictation					🕙 10 min

🗩 Chunking

For this lesson, your student will need to chunk:

<u>vowel chunks</u>   <u>consonant chunks</u>

What do bats eat? Some bats eat fruit or nectar from flowers. Most bats eat bugs. One bat can eat hundreds of bugs in just one night. That's a lot of bugs! Just think how many more bugs would be in the world if there were no bats!

<u>vowel chunks</u>: 8   <u>consonant chunks</u>: 6

🔊 Dictation

What do bats eat? Some bats eat fruit or nectar from flowers. Most bats eat bugs. One bat can eat hundreds of bugs in just one night. That's a lot of bugs! Just think how many more bugs would be in the world if there were no bats!

Word Count: 48

Lesson 22 Bossy *r* Chunks

	22A	22B	22C	22D	22E
📖 Shared Reading	✓	✓	✓	✓	✓
💬 Chunking	▇	▇	▇	▇	▇
✏️ Copywork	⏱ 10 min	⏱ 10 min	⏱ 10 min		
✨ No Rule Day				✓	
🔊 Dictation					⏱ 10 min

💬 Chunking

For this lesson, your student will need to chunk:

Bossy *r* chunks

Sometimes you will see Bossy *r* chunks called *r-controlled vowels*. The *r* "bosses," or changes, the sound of the vowel that precedes it. Because several vowels make the same sound when bossed by *r*, we recommend marking these chunks before everything but vowel chunks when marking more than one kind of letter pattern. This week, focus on Bossy *r* chunks exclusively.

A beav**er**'s home looks like a pile of sticks in a stream. Beav**er**s **are** good build**er**s. Using th**eir** sh**ar**p teeth, they gnaw through tree branches. Then they use the branches to build a dam. The dam makes a pond. The beav**er** builds a house in the pond. The do**or** to the house is und**er** wat**er**!

Bossy *r* chunks: 10

🔊 Dictation

A beaver's home looks like a pile of sticks in a stream. Beavers are good builders. Using their sharp teeth, they gnaw through tree branches. Then they use the branches to build a dam. The dam makes a pond. The beaver builds a house in the pond. The door to the house is under water!

Word Count: 55

Lesson 23 Vowel, Bossy *r*, and Consonant Chunks

	23A	23B	23C	23D	23E
📖 Shared Reading	✓	✓	✓	✓	✓
💬 Chunking					
✏️ Copywork	⏱ 10 min	⏱ 10 min	⏱ 10 min		
✨ No Rule Day				✓	
🔊 Dictation					⏱ 10 min

📖 Shared Reading

Just for fun: Can you and your student find a pair of words in the passage that rhyme? Here are some hints: 1) Each word is in the passage twice. 2) Each word includes two different kinds of chunks. 3) One word contains the other.*

Answer: The rhyming words are mother *and* other.

💬 Chunking

For this lesson, your student will need to chunk:

<u>vowel chunks</u>   **<u>Bossy *r* chunks</u>**   <u>consonant chunks</u>

Now your student will mark all three of the recently reviewed chunks. The recommended order is to first mark vowel, then Bossy *r*, then consonant chunks, but take this opportunity to discuss with your student the order that makes the most sense to them. If there are overlapping chunks, they should mark the chunks that they feel will be the most difficult for them to remember. Adjust the total numbers of each chunk as necessary.

The king penguin does not build a nest like other birds. The mother king penguin lays just one egg. She puts the egg on top of her feet. Then she folds a flap of skin over it to keep it warm. The mother and father take turns holding the egg. One holds it while the other looks for food.

vowel chunks: 9   Bossy *r* chunks: 11   consonant chunks: 18

🔊 Dictation

The king penguin does not build a nest like other birds. The mother king penguin lays just one egg. She puts the egg on top of her feet. Then she folds a flap of skin over it to keep it warm. The mother and father take turns holding the egg. One holds it while the other looks for food.

Word Count: 59

Lesson 24　Vowel, Bossy *r*, and Consonant Chunks

	24A	24B	24C	24D	24E
📖 Shared Reading	✓	✓	✓	✓	✓
💬 Chunking					
✏️ Copywork	⏱ 10 min	⏱ 10 min	⏱ 10 min		
✨ No Rule Day				✓	
🔊 Dictation					⏱ 10 min

💬 Chunking

For this lesson, your student will need to chunk:

vowel chunks　　Bossy *r* chunks　　consonant chunks

When vowel and Bossy *r* chunks overlap, as in the word *their*, we recommend marking the vowel chunk. If your student finds it more helpful to mark the Bossy *r* chunk, remember to adjust the total for each chunk when checking the answer key.

Most people know a raccoon by its mask. Raccoons also have paws that look like hands.
They use their paws for climbing and catching food. They can even pull lids off trash cans!
A raccoon's paws are very handy.

vowel chunks: 13　Bossy *r* chunks: 3　consonant chunks: 12

🔊 Dictation

Most people know a raccoon by its mask. Raccoons also have paws that look like hands.
They use their paws for climbing and catching food. They can even pull lids off trash cans!
A raccoon's paws are very handy.

Word Count: 39

	25A	25B	25C	25D	25E
📖 Shared Reading	✓	✓	✓	✓	✓
💬 Chunking					
✏️ Copywork	⏱ 10 min	⏱ 10 min	⏱ 10 min		
🪄 No Rule Day				✓	
🔊 Dictation					⏱ 10 min

💬 Chunking

For this lesson, your student will need to chunk:

vowel chunks   **Bossy *r* chunks**   **consonant chunks**   **silent letters**

The silent letter *e* in *slides* is not marked because, in this program, we include it as part of the ending *-es*. Silent letters are only marked if they are not part of other chunks. If your student identifies and marks it as a silent letter, do not mark it incorrect; consider it an opportunity to discuss their choice.

Remember to mark *qu* as a consonant chunk. Although it is a consonant-vowel combination, we have chosen to include it with the consonant chunks. In English spelling, the letter *q* is almost always followed by *u*.

A porcupine's quills lie flat until it is scared. Then they stand straight up! If something touches a porcupine, quills come loose. A quill slides easily into an enemy's skin. On the tip of the quill are rows of tiny, sharp hooks. They hold the quill in when it is pulled. Ouch!

vowel chunks: 10   Bossy *r* chunks: 5   consonant chunks: 23   silent letters: 6

🔊 Dictation

A porcupine's quills lie flat until it is scared. Then they stand straight up! If something touches a porcupine, quills come loose. A quill slides easily into an enemy's skin. On the tip of the quill are rows of tiny, sharp hooks. They hold the quill in when it is pulled. Ouch!

Word Count: 52

	26A	26B	26C	26D	26E
📖 Shared Reading	✓	✓	✓	✓	✓
💬 Chunking					
✏️ Copywork	⏱ 10 min	⏱ 10 min	⏱ 10 min		
🪄 No Rule Day				✓	
🔊 Dictation					⏱ 10 min

💬 Chunking

For this lesson, your student will need to chunk:

vowel chunks   **Bossy *r* chunks**   **consonant chunks**   **silent letters**

Mark silent letters after all other chunks are marked. Remember, even though they do not make a sound themselves, these silent letters affect the sounds that other letters make—and they can completely change the meaning of a word. Notice the difference between *on* and *one*. With the addition of just one silent *e* the *o* sound is completely different and the resulting word is, too.

A great white shark has a huge mouth. It is filled with rows of teeth. When a shark has lost one tooth, another tooth will move up to fill the empty space. A shark will have thousands of teeth over its lifetime.

vowel chunks: 8   Bossy *r* chunks: 5   consonant chunks: 18   silent letters: 8

🔊 Dictation

A great white shark has a huge mouth. It is filled with rows of teeth. When a shark has lost one tooth, another tooth will move up to fill the empty space. A shark will have thousands of teeth over its lifetime.

Word Count: 42

	27A	27B	27C	27D	27E
📖 Shared Reading	✓	✓	✓	✓	✓
💬 Chunking					
✏️ Copywork	⏱ 10 min	⏱ 10 min	⏱ 10 min		
🪄 No Rule Day				✓	
🔊 Dictation					⏱ 10 min

💬 Chunking

For this lesson, your student will need to chunk:

vowel chunks **Bossy *r* chunks** **consonant chunks** **endings** **silent letters**

In this lesson your student will be marking five of the letter patterns they have studied. We suggest marking them in the following order: vowels, Bossy *r*, consonants, endings, and silent letters. Students should make multiple passes through the passage, marking only one type of chunk at a time.

The passage does include two overlapping chunks. They are found in: *really*, where we have marked the ending *-ly* rather than the consonant chunk *ll*; and in *enemies*, where the ending *-es* is marked rather than the vowel chunk *ie*. Refer to page 35 for information on overlapping chunks.

Students may wonder why we have marked *-ly* in *really* but *ll* in *jellyfish*. If they are curious, here's the explanation: If you remove the letters *ly* from *jelly*, the remaining letters are not a word. The word *jelly* is a noun, spelled with the consonant chunk *ll*. The word *really* consists of the word *real* (an adjective) plus the ending *-ly*; together, these parts make an adverb. The effect that endings have on base words, including how spelling of the base word may change, will be introduced in *Ancient Achievements* and thoroughly covered in *Modern Milestones*.

Jellyfish are not really fish. The jellyfish looks like an umbrella. Long tentacles hang down. Be careful! Tentacles give a shock! Jellyfish use their tentacles for catching food and fighting enemies.

vowel chunks: 5   Bossy *r* chunks: 3   consonant chunks: 14   endings: 8   silent letters: 5

🔊 Dictation

Jellyfish are not really fish. The jellyfish looks like an umbrella. Long tentacles hang down. Be careful! Tentacles give a shock! Jellyfish use their tentacles for catching food and fighting enemies.

Word Count: 31

	28A	28B	28C	28D	28E
📖 Shared Reading	✓	✓	✓	✓	✓
💬 Chunking					
✏️ Copywork	⏱ 10 min	⏱ 10 min	⏱ 10 min		
✨ No Rule Day				✓	
🔊 Dictation					⏱ 10 min

💬 Chunking

For this lesson, your student will need to chunk:

vowel chunks   **Bossy *r* chunks**   **consonant chunks**   **Tricky *y* Guy**

Remember that Tricky *y* Guy can sound like long *e* (*baby*), long *i* (*fly*) or short *i* (*bicycle*).

Tricky *y* Guy doesn't have a colored reference box on the Student Workbook pages but should be marked with green.

When it is hot, do you play in water to cool off? Some kangaroos have a funny way of getting cool. They lick their furry arms until they are wet. Then the air dries their fur. As the fur becomes dry, the kangaroo cools off.

vowel chunks: 14   Bossy *r* chunks: 8   consonant chunks: 14   Tricky *y* Guy: 3

🔊 Dictation

When it is hot, do you play in water to cool off? Some kangaroos have a funny way of getting cool. They lick their furry arms until they are wet. Then the air dries their fur. As the fur becomes dry, the kangaroo cools off.

Word Count: 45

	29A	29B	29C	29D	29E
📖 Shared Reading	✓	✓	✓	✓	✓
💬 Chunking					
✏️ Copywork	⏱ 10 min	⏱ 10 min	⏱ 10 min		
✨ No Rule Day				✓	
🔊 Dictation					⏱ 10 min

💬 Chunking

For this lesson, your student will need to chunk:

vowel chunks   **Bossy *r* chunks**   **consonant chunks**   **endings**   **silent letters**

Because only silent letters that are not part of other chunks should be marked, mark them last.

Silent letters do not have a colored reference box on the student activity pages.

The word *away* has two separate vowel chunks, *aw* and *ay*.

Can you guess how howler monkeys got their name? They howl in the morning and in the evening. People can hear the howls up to three miles away. Some people think the males are the loudest animals on land.

vowel chunks: 16   Bossy *r* chunks: 3   consonant chunks: 10   endings: 4   silent letters: 5

🔊 Dictation

Can you guess how howler monkeys got their name? They howl in the morning and in the evening. People can hear the howls up to three miles away. Some people think the males are the loudest animals on land.

Word Count: 39

Lesson 30   Vowel, Bossy *r*, and Consonant Chunks; Silent Letters

	30A	30B	30C	30D	30E
📖 Shared Reading	✓	✓	✓	✓	✓
💬 Chunking					
✏️ Copywork	⏱ 10 min	⏱ 10 min	⏱ 10 min		
✨ No Rule Day				✓	
🔊 Dictation					⏱ 10 min

💬 Chunking

For this lesson, your student will need to chunk:

vowel chunks   **Bossy *r* chunks**   **consonant chunks**   **silent letters**

The word *squirrel* has several overlapping chunks. We have deviated from our suggested order for chunking and have marked the consonant chunk *qu* and the Bossy *r* chunk *ir*. Your student may chose to mark the vowel chunk *ui* or the consonant chunk *rr*. Point out the overlapping chunks and adjust the total numbers of chunks as necessary. You may wish to discuss these overlapping chunks before your student begins marking them.

Remember that *qu* is marked as a consonant chunk.

Squirrels around the world use their tails in many ways. Tails can help them balance in trees. When some squirrels are scared, they fluff and wave their tails to look bigger and stronger. When it is cold, a squirrel can use its tail to keep warm. When it is hot, a squirrel can flip its tail over its back for shade.

vowel chunks: 13   Bossy *r* chunks: 13   consonant chunks: 16   silent letters: 7

🔊 Dictation

Squirrels around the world use their tails in many ways. Tails can help them balance in trees. When some squirrels are scared, they fluff and wave their tails to look bigger and stronger. When it is cold, a squirrel can use its tail to keep warm. When it is hot, a squirrel can flip its tail over its back for shade.

Word Count: 61

Lesson 31 All Letter Patterns

	31A	31B	31C	31D	31E
📖 Shared Reading	✓	✓	✓	✓	✓
💬 Chunking					
✏️ Copywork	⏱ 10 min	⏱ 10 min	⏱ 10 min		
✨ No Rule Day				✓	
🔊 Dictation					⏱ 10 min

💬 Chunking

For this lesson, your student will need to chunk:

vowel chunks   Bossy *r* chunks   consonant chunks   Tricky *y* Guy   endings   silent letters

For the remaining lessons in this level, your student will mark all of the letter patterns they have learned. It is recommended to mark the chunks in the suggested order to avoid confusion. See page 35 for information on chunking order. Remember that students should only mark one type of chunk at a time and make multiple passes through the passage. If your student struggles to mark all of the chunks in less than 10 minutes or so, see page 35 for suggestions on how to make chunking less stressful.

Did you ever fix dinner while floating on your back? That's what the sea otter does. It gathers clams and puts them into pouches under its front legs. Then it swims to the surface. As it floats, the otter puts a flat rock on its chest. It knocks the clam against the rock to open it. Dinner's ready!

vowel chunks: 9   Bossy *r* chunks: 8   consonant chunks: 22   Tricky *y* Guy: 1   endings: 2   silent letters: 2

🔊 Dictation

Did you ever fix dinner while floating on your back? That's what the sea otter does. It gathers clams and puts them into pouches under its front legs. Then it swims to the surface. As it floats, the otter puts a flat rock on its chest. It knocks the clam against the rock to open it. Dinner's ready!

Word Count: 58

Lesson 32 All Letter Patterns

	32A	32B	32C	32D	32E
📖 Shared Reading	✓	✓	✓	✓	✓
💬 Chunking					
✏️ Copywork	⏱ 10 min	⏱ 10 min	⏱ 10 min		
✨ No Rule Day				✓	
🔊 Dictation					⏱ 10 min

💬 Chunking

For this lesson, your student will need to chunk:

vowel chunks   **Bossy *r* chunks**   **consonant chunks**   **Tricky *y* Guy**   **endings**   **silent letters**

A honeybee finds a new patch of flowers. What does it do? The bee flies back to the hive and starts dancing. The way it moves shows where the food is. The number of times the bee shakes its body tells how far away the food is. Soon the other bees are on their way!

vowel chunks: 19   Bossy *r* chunks: 7   consonant chunks: 17   Tricky *y* Guy: 1   endings: 4   silent letters: 3

✨ No Rule Day

Your student may wish to draw a map or write directions to a "treasure" of their choice. Or, like the bees, they may choose to dance their directions! Presenting instructions in a logical sequence is a valuable skill to develop.

🔊 Dictation

A honeybee finds a new patch of flowers. What does it do? The bee flies back to the hive and starts dancing. The way it moves shows where the food is. The number of times the bee shakes its body tells how far away the food is. Soon the other bees are on their way!

Word Count: 55

Lesson 33   All Letter Patterns

	33A	33B	33C	33D	33E
📖 Shared Reading	✓	✓	✓	✓	✓
💬 Chunking					
✏️ Copywork	⏱ 10 min	⏱ 10 min	⏱ 10 min		
✨ No Rule Day				✓	
🔊 Dictation					⏱ 10 min

💬 Chunking

For this lesson, your student will need to chunk:

vowel chunks   Bossy *r* chunks   consonant chunks   Tricky *y* Guy   endings   silent letters

In the word *quickly*, as with other *qu* words, we have chosen to mark the consonant chunk *qu* rather than the vowel chunk *ui*. *Q* is not a frequently used consonant; in fact, *q* is the second least frequently used letter in words of English origin! (Can you guess what the least frequently used letter is?*) We choose to chunk *qu* rather than the vowel chunk following it to emphasize that *q* is, with the exception of a handful of words, always followed by *u* in English words. The *qu* chunk is always followed by another vowel in English words. If your student chooses to mark the vowel chunk, remember to adjust the totals when checking their work.

Did you guess? The least frequently used letter in English words is z. Do you know any words that are spelled with a z?

Many woodpeckers use their beaks for making holes in tree trunks. They look for tunnels made by bugs under the bark. When the woodpecker finds a tunnel, it pecks a small hole. It quickly puts its long tongue inside. The tongue is sticky and has hooks on the end for catching bugs. The bird can also eat bugs that scurry out of the holes.

vowel chunks: 12   Bossy *r* chunks: 8   consonant chunks: 21   Tricky *y* Guy: 4

endings: 5   silent letters: 4

🔊 Dictation

Many woodpeckers use their beaks for making holes in tree trunks. They look for tunnels made by bugs under the bark. When the woodpecker finds a tunnel, it pecks a small hole. It quickly puts its long tongue inside. The tongue is sticky and has hooks on the end for catching bugs. The bird can also eat bugs that scurry out of the holes.

Word Count: 64

	34A	34B	34C	34D	34E
📖 Shared Reading	✓	✓	✓	✓	✓
💬 Chunking					
✏️ Copywork	⏱ 10 min	⏱ 10 min	⏱ 10 min		
✨ No Rule Day				✓	
🔊 Dictation					⏱ 10 min

📖 Shared Reading

Just for fun: Compound words are words that are made up of two smaller words. When the two words are combined into one, the new word has a different meaning from either of the two smaller ones. *Seahorse* is a compound word made up of the smaller words *sea* and *horse*. Can you find another compound word in this passage?*

*Answer: Upright *is a compound word made of the smaller words* up *and* right.

💬 Chunking

For this lesson, your student will need to chunk:

vowel chunks   **Bossy *r* chunks**   **consonant chunks**   **Tricky *y* Guy**   **endings**   **silent letters**

Seahorses are fish, but they are not like other fish. Seahorses swim upright. They have a curved neck. They do not have scales. Their fins are very small, so they swim poorly. A seahorse uses its tail to hold onto sea grasses. A group of seahorses is called a herd—just like a herd of horses!

vowel chunks: 13   Bossy *r* chunks: 13   consonant chunks: 13   Tricky *y* Guy: 1
endings: 10   silent letters: 8

🔊 Dictation

Seahorses are fish, but they are not like other fish. Seahorses swim upright. They have a curved neck. They do not have scales. Their fins are very small, so they swim poorly. A seahorse uses its tail to hold onto sea grasses. A group of seahorses is called a herd—just like a herd of horses!

Word Count: 56

Lesson 35 All Letter Patterns

	35A	35B	35C	35D	35E
📖 Shared Reading	✓	✓	✓	✓	✓
💬 Chunking					
✏️ Copywork	⏱ 10 min	⏱ 10 min	⏱ 10 min		
✨ No Rule Day				✓	
🔊 Dictation					⏱ 10 min

💬 Chunking

For this lesson, your student will need to chunk:

vowel chunks   **Bossy _r_ chunks**   **consonant chunks**   **Tricky _y_ Guy**   **endings**   **silent letters**

The word _babie_s has an overlapping chunk. We have chosen to mark the vowel chunk _ie_, but your student may choose to mark the ending _-es_. This is fine. Whichever they choose, point out the other choice and adjust the total number of each chunk if necessary.

There is a sneaky silent _b_ in this passage—be alert!

When it is time to lay eggs, a crocodile mother makes a nest. She might dig a hole by a river. When they hatch, the babies call to their mother. They cannot climb out of the hole. The mother picks them up gently in her mouth. Then she carries them to the water.

vowel chunks: 8   Bossy _r_ chunks: 7   consonant chunks: 24   Tricky _y_ Guy: 1
endings: 2   silent letters: 5

🔊 Dictation

When it is time to lay eggs, a crocodile mother makes a nest. She might dig a hole by a river. When they hatch, the babies call to their mother. They cannot climb out of the hole. The mother picks them up gently in her mouth. Then she carries them to the water.

Word Count: 53

	36A	36B	36C	36D	36E
📖 Shared Reading	✓	✓	✓	✓	✓
💬 Chunking					
✏️ Copywork	⏱ 10 min	⏱ 10 min	⏱ 10 min		
✨ No Rule Day				✓	
🔊 Dictation					⏱ 10 min

📖 Shared Reading

Just for fun: Find a video of a giant panda crunching bamboo. Then compare it to how you and your student sound crunching celery!

💬 Chunking

For this lesson, your student will need to chunk:

vowel chunks   **Bossy _r_ chunks**   **consonant chunks**   **Tricky _y_ Guy**   **endings**   **silent letters**

The giant panda is a kind of bear. It lives in the country of China. Tall bamboo plants grow there. This is mostly what the giant panda eats. The panda has to eat a lot of bamboo. Giant pandas spend about half of each day just eating!

vowel chunks: 14   Bossy _r_ chunks: 1   consonant chunks: 10   Tricky _y_ Guy: 1
endings: 3   silent letters: 2

🔊 Dictation

The giant panda is a kind of bear. It lives in the country of China. Tall bamboo plants grow there. This is mostly what the giant panda eats. The panda has to eat a lot of bamboo. Giant pandas spend about half of each day just eating!

Word Count: 47

Celebrate!

This is the very last lesson in *Wild Tales*. Your student has learned so much about spelling and letter patterns, plus some fun and interesting facts about animals. Congratulations to both of you on a job well done!

Next Steps

Americana is the next level of Spelling You See. It uses interesting passages about American history and culture to continue reinforcing and expanding spelling skills in the skill development stage.

Frequently Asked Questions

? Are students allowed to ask for help?

Yes. It is a positive step when students articulate their questions. Encourage your student to ask if they are confused by something. For example, if they aren't sure whether *cab* starts with *c* or *k*, have them ask rather than write the word incorrectly. You want your student to succeed, so help them by eliminating opportunities for mistakes. It is better for a student to have the visual image of the correct letter or word rather than an incorrect one.

? In lessons where chunks overlap, which one should my student mark?

Some words will have overlapping chunks or letter patterns. Look at the focus of the lesson to see which one you should choose. For example, if the focus is consonant chunks, mark the *ll* in *finally*. If the focus is endings, then the *-ly* should be marked.

In lessons where several chunks are to be marked, we recommend that students follow the suggested order for chunking provided on page 35. However, do not consider it wrong if the student chooses a different chunk to mark. Discuss their choice and point out other possible choices. See page 35 for more detailed information on overlapping chunks.

? My student wants to do their copywork in cursive. Is this okay?

No. Copywork should be printed in order to develop visual memory. When students read, everything they see is in print, so they should use printing while learning to spell. Save cursive for written work in other subjects.

? Should my student erase during copywork or passage dictation?

Students should erase during copywork, if necessary, so that they copy the words correctly. When students are completing dictation, however, it is important not to erase. If you notice an error being made, allow your student to complete the word before providing feedback. Don't stop the clock, though! Give your student examples of different spellings, if needed, in order to see which one looks right. See About the Activities: Dictation for examples of how to do this. Then simply have them draw a line through the incorrect spelling and continue with the passage.

? Should I keep a list of words that my student misses?

No, this is not necessary. Words that are commonly misspelled will come up again in future lessons. This program encourages visual memory, not rote memory.

Frequently Asked Questions

**(?) There are no spelling tests with this program.
How can I tell if my student is making progress?**

Look for your student's ability to complete a dictation page with increasing speed and accuracy. You should also begin to see more accurate spelling in other daily work. Each child will progress through the developmental process at their own pace, so be patient and do not put pressure on your student. If you are required to or would like to keep a portfolio of your student's work, pages may be removed from the workbooks at regular intervals and kept in a folder. Be sure not to treat dictation exercises as tests.

(?) My student doesn't seem to be making progress. Do you have any suggestions?

Some students have trouble hearing sounds clearly, possibly because of auditory processing delays or a history of ear infections. Whatever the reason for slow progress, do not be tempted to skip ahead. Review the guidelines and tips in this Handbook and watch the instructional videos to ensure that you are completing the activities properly and giving your student the best chance for success. If your student is having trouble with words that follow regular phonetic patterns, such as *cat* or *dog*, you may want to consider using the previous level, *Jack and Jill*, first.

(?) My student does fine in their spelling book and when they're copying word for word. If they write something on their own, though, their spelling is horrible. Why?

Copying and creating are two very different activities for the brain. Copywork and dictation help the student develop a visual memory, as the brain is focusing on the way the words actually look in print. When a student is creating a story, their brain is operating differently. It takes a long time for spelling to become implanted and automatic. Until that happens, you will continue to see spelling errors in your student's free writing. That is why consistent copying of the same passage multiple times is so critical. At the same time, continue to give your student plenty of opportunities for free writing without correcting their spelling. This will nurture their creativity and will not negatively impact their spelling education.

Frequently Asked Questions

(?) My student struggles with dictation. They make many errors and are weak in self-correction. We have been following all of the guidelines for dictation but it does not seem to be getting any easier. We are both getting frustrated. What can we do? Should we just keep pressing on and hope it gets better?

There are some modifications you can make for students who struggle with the process of dictation. It is possible that your student is simply experiencing too many things to focus on. Rather than trying to push through the complete passage, try limiting dictation to just the first sentence. Provide dictation word by word for just this sentence. Repeat the same sentence if it is completed within the ten-minute time frame.

Sit next to—not across from—your student during dictation time and observe their efforts. As soon as a mistake is noticed or your student asks for help, stop and help them find the correct spelling. For example, suggest that they try writing the word with and without an *e* at the end, and then choose the one that looks right. If they don't come up with the correct spelling themselves and are beginning to get frustrated, write a couple of options yourself on a separate piece of paper. Say, "Here are a couple of options: *wen* or *when*. Which looks right?" Then have them copy the correct spelling. Count their correct choice as a correct word when totaling the number of words spelled correctly. Don't stop the clock while you're doing this.

Make sure that you are completing the other lesson activities of reading aloud to each other, chunking, and copywork. Repeated exposure to the passage will increase your student's familarity with spelling and letter patterns and increase their visual memory.

Finally, remember that the goal of dictation is not to complete the entire passage, but to spell as many words correctly, as comfortably as possible, in ten minutes. As your student gains confidence and masters a single, repeated sentence for several weeks, consider adding the second sentence of the weekly passage, and so on until you are using the entire passage. If that never happens, that's okay too. Dictation is simply an opportunity to show you and themselves what they have internalized from the other weekly activities.

(?) I love the approach of Spelling You See, but my student and I have color vision deficiency. The program uses color chunking as an essential activity, but we can't distinguish between some of the colors. Is there a way we can still use the program?

Yes, you can. We offer a symbol-coded answer key for the chunking sections. You can download this from the Digital Tools section on spellingyousee.com. Instructions for how to use symbol marking for chunking can also be found there. None of the other activities require distinguishing between colors.

Blend

Two or more consonants that appear together but keep their distinct sounds. Words like *flag*, *stop*, and *stream* begin with blends, and the word *fast* ends with a blend. A blend is different than a consonant chunk because all the sounds of the consonants are heard.

Bossy *r*

A letter pattern in which a vowel is followed by an *r* that controls ("bosses") the vowel by changing its sound. Bossy *r* chunks are always marked with purple in Spelling You See.

Chunk

A particular letter pattern that occurs frequently in English and which may or may not have a predictable sound.

Chunking

The process of finding and marking all designated letter patterns in a particular passage.

Consonant

Any letter of the alphabet that is not a vowel. The consonants are *b, c, d, f, g, h, j, k, l, m, n, p, q, r, s, t, v, w, x, y*, and *z*.

Consonant Chunks

A combination of two or more consonants that together make a single sound. Consonant chunks may also be silent. Consonant chunks are always marked with blue in Spelling You See.

Copywork

Words or sentences provided for a student to copy.

Decode

Use letter-to-sound correspondence to read a word in print (reading).

Dictation

The process of reading a sentence or passage aloud and having the student write it without looking at the passage while accessing their visual memory.

Encode

Create a word from individual sounds (spelling).

Endings

Letters added to the end of a base word to change its meaning. Examples are *-ly* and *-ing*. Endings are always marked with pink or red in Spelling You See.

High-Frequency Words

The most commonly used words, such as *the*, *and*, or *but*. Many high-frequency words are not spelled phonetically; see *sight words*.

Phonemic Awareness

The ability to distinguish the individual sounds that make up spoken words.

Phonics

The study of the sounds usually indicated by letters and combinations of letters in a particular language.

Sight Words

High-frequency words that are non-phonetic and, as a result, are especially challenging for emerging readers. Examples are *come*, *look*, *of*, *said*, and *some*.

Silent Letter

A letter that is included when spelling a word but that has no sound when the word is pronounced. The letter may change the pronunciation of the word (e.g., *cut*, *cute*). Silent letters are always marked with orange in Spelling You See.

Syllable

A word or part of a word pronounced as a single unit. It consists of one vowel sound and often the consonant sounds that cluster around it.

Tricky *y* Guy

A *y* in the middle or at the end of a word that is sounded as a vowel instead of as a consonant. Examples include *bicycle* and *why*. Tricky *y* Guy is always marked with green in Spelling You See.

Vowel

One of the letters *a*, *e*, *i*, *o*, and *u*. Sometimes *y* and *w* may act as vowels. Every syllable and word in the English language has at least one vowel sound.

Vowel Chunks

A combination of two or more vowels. A vowel chunk usually makes a single sound. The letters *y* and *w* may act as vowels and be included as part of a vowel chunk. Vowel chunks are always marked with yellow in Spelling You See.

Index of Topics   A–I

Index of Topics J–Z

Bibliography

This curriculum is based on years of research into how children learn to read and spell. Here are some of the resources that were used in the development of this program.

Berk, L. E., & Winsler, A. (1995). *Scaffolding children's learning: Vygotsky and early childhood education.* Washington, DC: National Association for the Education of Young Children.

Clay, M. M. (2015). *Becoming literate: The construction of inner control.* Portsmouth, NH: Heinemann.

Clay, M. M. (2010). *What changes in writing can I see?* Portsmouth, NH: Heinemann.

Cook, D. L. (2004). *When your child struggles: The myths of 20/20 vision: What every parent needs to know.* Atlanta, GA: Invision Press.

Cunningham, P. (2016). *Phonics they use: Words for reading and writing.* (7th ed.). Boston, MA: Pearson Education.

Flanigan, K., Hayes, L., Templeton, S., Bear, D. R., Invernizzi, M. R., & Johnston, F. (2011). *Words their way with struggling readers: Word study for reading, vocabulary, and spelling instruction, grades 4–12.* Boston, MA: Allyn & Bacon.

Ganske, K. (2013). *Word journeys: Assessment-guided phonics, spelling, and vocabulary instruction.* (2nd ed.). New York, NY: Guilford Press.

Heilman, A. W. (2006). *Phonics in proper perspective.* (10th ed.). Pearson Education.

Henderson, E. H. (1990). *Teaching spelling.* (2nd ed.). Boston, MA: Houghton Mifflin.

Levine, M. (2000). *Educational care: A system for understanding and helping children with learning differences at home and in school* (2nd ed.). Cambridge, MA: Educators Publishing Service.

Lyons, C. A. (2003). *Teaching struggling readers: How to use brain-based research to maximize learning.* Portsmouth, NH: Heinemann.

McCarrier, A., Pinnell, G. S., & Fountas, I. C. (2000). *Interactive writing: How language and literacy come together, K–2.* Portsmouth, NH: Heinemann.

Pinnell, G. S., & Fountas, I. C. (2018). *Word matters: Teaching phonics and spelling in the reading/writing classroom.* Portsmouth, NH: Heinemann.

Read, C. (1971). Pre-school children's knowledge of English phonology. *Harvard Educational Review, 41*(1), 150–179.

Sprenger, M. (1999). *Learning and memory: The brain in action.* Alexandria, VA: Association for Supervision and Curriculum Development.

Wood, D. (2012). *How children think and learn: The social contexts of cognitive development.* Cambridge, MA: Blackwell Publishers.

Zutell, J. (2006). Word sorting: A developmental spelling approach to word study for delayed readers. *Reading and Writing Quarterly, 14*(2), 219–238.